This book belongs to

_____

It is all about a kitten named

_____

It was started on

_____

My Kitten's
Baby Book

A Special Book of Kitten Memories and Milestones

A Brolly Book

Place a kitten photograph here.

I was born...

The date
_____

[insert approximate date if actual date not known]

The place
_____

[insert approximate place if actual date not known]

My gender
_____

My breed
_____

Other things about me at this time
_____

_____

_____

I came home to my people family...

On
_____

To
_____

My people family named me
_____

Because
_____

Other special things about me
_____

_____

A Pocket full of Memories

The perfect place for
locks of fur, special photos, journal notes,
letters and cards to your kitten, small mementoes
such as name tags and kitten collars, certificates, family tree and breeding
notes, growth charts, and more. Slip them in here for safe-keeping,
and be sure to individually bag and label them if
you need to first.

Place a kitten photograph here.

When I came home . . .

My fur was
_____

[describe fur: long, short, curly, soft, wiry, the colour, etc.]

The colour of my eyes was
_____

My ears were
_____

[describe ears: big, small, pointy, the colour, etc.]

The length of my body was
_____

[measure from the base of the tail to the 'withers', the highest point of the shoulders]

My height was
_____

[measure from ground to withers]

My entire length from the tip of my nose to the tip of my tail was
_____

[always measure gently and carefully and if your kitten does not want you to, stop immediately!]

My weight was
_____

9

Friends and family

People in my animal family
_____

_____

Animals in my animal family
_____

_____

Use this page for photographs

My favourite things

Food
_____

Drink
_____

Toys
_____

Games
_____

Time of day
_____

because
_____

_____

My favourite things

Place to play inside

Place to play outside

Place to sleep inside

Place to sleep outside

Place to sit inside

Place to sit outside

Favourite photos

The first time I . . .

Was groomed

_____

Did something on command, when I . . .

_____

[note: for a cat, the answer could be 'Never!']

Went to the vet

_____

Washed myself

_____

Miaowed

_____

Purred

_____

Other firsts

_____

My first friends

My first friends were

I met them at

Things I did with my first friends

More Favourite photos

Mischief that I got up to

Things that I did . . .

Special events and adventures

Things I did and saw . . .

Me and my moods

When I am happy I . . .

When I am sad I . . .

When I am cross I . . .

When I am excited I . . .

When I am tired I . . .

When I am hungry I . . .

When I want your attention I . . .

A Pocket full of Memories

The perfect place for
locks of fur, special photos, journal notes,
letters and cards to your kitten, small mementoes
such as name tags and kitten collars, certificates, family tree and breeding
notes, growth charts, and more. Slip them in here for safe-keeping,
and be sure to individually bag and label them if
you need to first.

Place a kitten photograph here.

Things I taught my family

_____

[for example, when to feed me, open the door for me, make up my bed]

_____

Things my family taught me

_____

[note: for cats, the answer could be 'Nothing!'— they are very clever and knowing.]

_____

Special tricks that I do

_____

_____

23

My health records

Vaccinations and treatments*	Due by	Completed

Other medical and health notes about me (including allergies)

24   * Include all essential vaccinations as well as additional treatments and vaccinations for flea control, worming, etc.

Vital Information

Microchip number:

Council registration number:

Council registration/renewal due:

Vet's name and contact number:

Veterinary hospital name, address, and number:

In case of emergency, contact: